Even More Concise

10 Second Sermons

Even More Concise 10 Second Sermons

Milton Jones

DARTON · LONGMAN + TODD

First published in 2013 by
Darton, Longman and Todd Ltd
1 Spencer Court
140 – 142 Wandsworth High Street
London SW18 4JJ

ISBN: 978-0-232-53004-9

A catalogue record for this book is available from the British Library

Designed and produced by Judy Linard
Printed and bound in Great Britain by
Page Bros, Norwich, Norfolk

Contents

For all those who are genuinely searching,
but also have a really short attention span.
Assuming you've read this far …

Thanks

Thankfulness is the best moisturiser
for a wrinkly personality.

MY TALK TODAY IS ON INTEGRITY
AND THE NEED TO AVOID PLAGIARISM
YOU MAY SAY I'M A DREAMER,
BUT I'M NOT THE ONLY ONE...

Here We Go

Suppose it's all a lot bigger than anyone thinks or can even imagine.

Okay, I'm telling you now …

IT

IS.

Warning to self

Don't point out the fleck of soup in your neighbour's beard if there's an upside-down bowl of spaghetti bolognese on your own head.

Introduction

So we all agree then, both good and bad has been done in the name of religion? So maybe the bigger question is: How do we know what is good and what is bad?

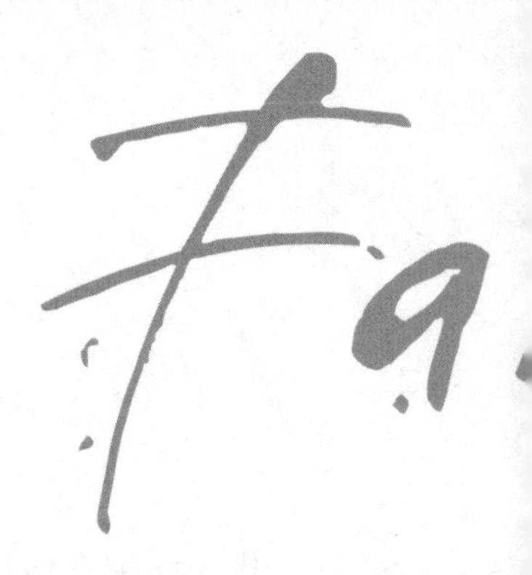

Unfortunately for those of us who like to look stylish and enigmatic, the Christian faith is embarrassingly simple.

If becoming a Christian is *just* about changing your culture and language, I may as well become a Norwegian.

One of the mysteries of Christianity is why Christians rarely admit that so much of it is a mystery.

Apart from being involved at the beginning of science, systems of government, philosophy, art, schools, hospitals, the emancipation of women, the abolition of slavery, social welfare, helping form the basis of the moral code most people live by, and introducing popular notions of justice, mercy, peace, decency and compassion what has christianity ever done for the world?

People who have faith for a big thing have usually had faith for many smaller things.

Having a Christian faith cannot be like paying into some sort of pension scheme where you get eternal life in exchange for an hour of boredom every week. It has to be more like being a part-time lightning conductor.

Or being a Christian has to be more like being on fire. So, if I only have a 'private faith' then maybe I'm the only one who can feel the warmth of my 'flames'?

I THINK SOME PEOPLE HERE HAVE TROUBLE WITH THEIR IDENTITY... YOU KNOW WHO YOU ARE....

God

SO.. HE JUST LETS
THEM OFF? ...

APPARENTL

God can be a bit like someone called Jeff. When people talk about him you think you know who they mean, but in reality they might be talking about someone else who they call Jeff.

Some people say that God doesn't exist because they don't understand his actions. But then I have no idea what air-traffic controllers, earthworms or morris dancers are up to, and most people seem to believe they all exist …

God cannot be like a Yeti or the Loch Ness Monster – an interesting myth that may or may not be true. God has to be more like the idea that black holes are gateways to other parts of the universe. If true, it changes everything!

So if God is like a traffic cop why doesn't he just let everyone off their penalty points? He does, but to get let off you have to admit you were in control of the vehicle at the time.

Do you ever wonder why God doesn't tell people clearly that: a) he exists, and b) what they need to do about it? But maybe he uses instinct not words, and many people don't get as far as b).

When something unfair happens, God often acts like a football referee who lets play continue to see if those wronged can gain some kind of advantage out of it.

God's love cannot be like a wedding cake, only bearable in small bites to bloated guests. It's more like the smell of fish and chips to a starving man.

God's Voice

(God says) beware of people who start their sentences with the words 'God says …'. They are either very wrong, or very right.

The quickest way to find out if there is an omnipresent God is to ask him if he exists, wherever you are.

Scientists say there could be up to seventeen billion earth-sized planets. So I'm pretty sure God doesn't mind what flavour crisps you choose.

The universe cannot be described as an accident, because 'accidents' can only happen when you know what *should* happen.

I wonder if God invented evolution ... Sorry – too soon?

ACCIDENT

LAUGHTER, JOY, BEAUTY, EATING,
HOPE, MONKEYS, TREES, ICE CREAM
... ARE YOU SURE?... I MEAN..
ALL THAT....

...

God's creation is like him – inexplicably clever, outrageously excessive and a bit weird. Too many of us Christians just manage the 'a bit weird' part.

When you look at the size and diversity of the universe, how can one group of people know all the answers? But then equally, how can another group know that there are no answers at all?

What's rarely mentioned by either side in the creation versus evolution debate is that *it's not the most important thing.*

A lot of organised religion seems like a man who was told that the only thing he could give God was to be found in a mirror. So he went off and made God a hugely elaborate ornamental mirror.

Being involved in organised religion is like trying to thread a needle while wearing oven gloves. Inevitably it's clumsy, but at least someone's trying to sew asbestos patches on the trousers of life … which are clearly on fire!

Having a faith is a bit like visiting a stately home. Those who don't realise its historical significance head straight for the gift shop to see what they can get for themselves.

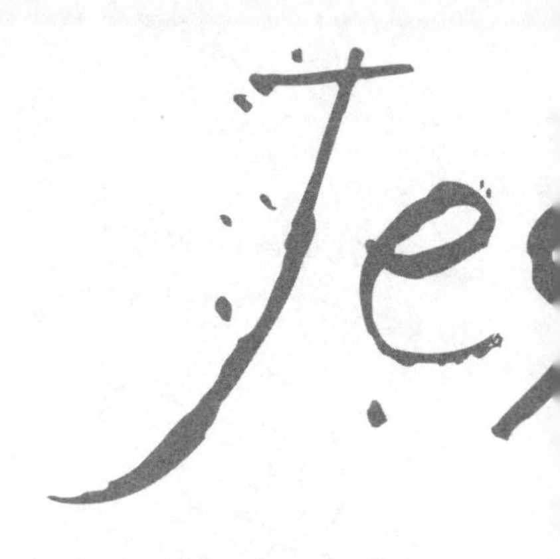

We are all born disconnected. Jesus is the adaptor.

'Knock Knock.'
'Who's there?'
'Jesus.'
'Jesus who?'
'The Jesus who even dares to speak through clichés ...'

GREAT TO HAVE YOU HERE JESUS, NOW PLEASE COULD YOU TELL EVERYONE REALLY CLEARLY HOW YOU BECAME A CHRISTIAN?..

So run it past me one more time: Jesus came to identify with the suffering of ordinary people, and now his chief 'representatives' live in huge palaces and wear big pointy hats?

Just an idea: church buildings should have a height restriction sign at the entrance, so that everyone has to enter on their knees.

When it works, church is like Lego – accommodating each other's nobbly bits makes us all stick together.

I wish doing good wasn't so often tainted by the knowledge that you can, or could, be asked to tell everyone about it later.

One of the Church's biggest battles is to remain an active fighting unit, and to resist becoming a battle re-enactment society.

If Christians are like sponges absorbing the mess of the world around them, then obviously the more effective they are, the more they will need a squeeze from time to time.

When church is boring it's either my fault, or it's not real church.

Perhaps think of different Christian denominations as pots, pans and improvised plastic containers, desperately flung out into the desert to try and catch any drops of rain.

Sometimes it's as if a few of us can't cope with the fact that if you really say 'sorry', he really does just let you off. So we have to make up other rules and special ways of talking, to sort of help punish everyone.

Best not to point out the tiny weed in your neighbour's garden if you have an old fridge, a stinking mattress and half a motorbike in yours.

It's an awkward fact that by definition a Christian God is always prepared to sacrifice something or someone for the greater good, no matter how inexplicable it might seem at the time.

If God speaks through church leaders, why does the idea of a sermon that lasts just ten seconds seem quite popular? (The reality may be different.)

God is light. But people prefer the limelight.

What's rarely mentioned by either side in the homosexuality debate is that *it's not the most important thing.*

Heaven

My Grandfather was an atheist, but now I should think he's up there somewhere … apologising.

I bet that arriving in Heaven won't be like going from main course to dessert, but more like going from milk to solids. (And that the reward system will be given out on an 'able to cope with' basis.)

Some gro

I just really, really hope God likes loud folk music.

The Pope's first tweet was 'Praise the Lord'. Perhaps it should have been 'OMG earth not centre of universe, soz Copernicus LOL'.

When it's good the Church of England is like a temporary hospital housed in a museum. When it's bad, it's like a medical museum with live exhibits recreating the full horror of how things used to be done in the old days.

ss of Believers

Why did the Baptist cross the road? It doesn't matter, as long as 'the cross' is mentioned.

Why did the chicken cross himself? Because he was relying mainly on superstition to get to the other side.

'BEFORE I SPEAK ABOUT WHY
CHRISTIANS NO LONGER
HAVE TO LIVE IN FEAR,
WHY DONT YOU TURN
TO THE PERSON NEXT
TO YOU AND SAY
HELLO?..'

If Christians are all different parts of one body, I've certainly met a few 'brains' who think, and some 'arms' that do the carrying – but also a disproportionate amount of 'appendixes' who don't appear to do anything at all, and some of whom will no doubt one day cause a lot of trouble. Perhaps I'm one of them.

If I ask God for something I might have to wait until I'm ready to receive it, and that could take ages. Or it might never happen at all.

Praying seems to be like trying to undo a knot. You never quite know what's going to work, it's just important to keep going. (Also, best check what you're trying to undo isn't holding up something else important.)

I WAS PRAYING AND A PAIR OF SCISSORS POPPED INTO MY HEAD

Christians

'Upholding Christian values' can be a way of insulating myself from the world, which is the ultimate un-Christian value.

Often when I ask God what he wants me to do next, I'm just trying to get out of what I'm supposed to be doing at the moment.

We are all like easily distracted dogs who run beyond the range of our master's shouts and whistles, making it a lot more complicated for him to follow us around with a plastic bag and trowel.

pious chart

Best to try and see the good in people, even if sometimes it's only manure that one day could sustain roses.

Effective Christians know they're flawed – travel bags with broken zips, tubs of butter with bits of toast in, small boats that need bailing out occasionally.

Too often I'm like a pigeon living in a railway station – oblivious of all those around making vital decisions about where to go and how to get there.

Judgement

The End will be like a bright light coming on a mile under the ocean – a lot of ugly monsters will suddenly be revealed.

NOW ARE YOU SURE YOU'VE GRASPED THE CONCEPT OF ETERNAL DAMNATION?'

Patience

LOVE IS PATIENT, LOVE IS KIND.. LOVE IS.. NEVER LATE!! YOU KNOW WE STARTED AT ELEVEN DONT YOU?

Meetings

Christian meetings are like going to the gym – good for building up strength but not much use if you just hang around and show off to the other members.

Once there was a man who was really interested in finding out the truth. He was willing to read and to listen to arguments, and perhaps even one day to make a decision to accept some sort of religion. Then he died.

Being saved is like being a fly buzzing around a room with no exit then someone gently guiding you to an open window, when in retrospect it would have been a lot easier just to squash you flat in the first place.

Being saved is to realise your company is bankrupt, but then to get an offer from a huge investor at the last moment. Obviously there will have to be changes, but incredibly they still want you to run the company!

ARE YOU SURE HE JUST LETS THEM OFF?...

MMMMM

'Knowing your theology' is just thinking that you're able to name the various parts of the engine of salvation. The main point, of course, is that it works.

False religions contain superstition, fear and abuse. Especially those within Christianity.

The Holy Grail of Christianity is not, as you might expect, the Holy Grail. But rather what it represents: to make and keep making the choice to give up your life for others.

Q: Should artists who are Christians just produce Christian art?

A: Should bakers who are Christians just produce hot cross buns?

Most atheists follow another famous atheist – a patron saint of atheism – who they don't pray to, obviously.

We all have a natural revulsion against evil, but if you're an atheist it's just harder to explain.

The main flaw of the science versus faith debate is the assumption that each side speaks with one voice.

SHOULDN'T IT BE THE 'CRUCIFACT'?

Sometimes it feels like the world has a deep internal injury, which only comes out on the surface as the bruises of pain and cruelty.

Sin is like a smashed glass that you thought you'd cleared up ages ago, but from time to time in dark corners you find the odd jaggedy bit. And if you don't deal with it, someone could get hurt.

Sin is like a drop off a cliff. We all have a compulsion to look over the edge, but if you fall it's worth remembering the pain of hitting the ground, and how long it can take to climb back up again.

Visualisation is imagining something happening so that when you get that opportunity in real life you don't hesitate to bring it about. Unfortunately it seems to work for bad thoughts as well as good ones.

We all have a breaking point, when the door flings open and either God or bad can step in. To be honest, there's often an undignified scuffle on the doorstep …

Coming from a Christian home is like receiving the antidote to a poison for your first birthday. You can't fully appreciate its worth until you've seen the effects of the poison at first hand.

The Greenland Shark can't swim as fast as a seal. But it succeeds by creeping up on those that are asleep, and then sucking the life out of them.

We are all like different types of car – in certain circumstances we will fail. So best not go down those roads, if you can avoid them.

But if for some reason you do have to lurch along one of those tracks, stay alert and tell a friend where you're going.

If I persistently avoid someone, then it's far easier to think of them as just a two-dimensional cartoon character. Meeting them unavoidably changes that.

If you keep fueling the vehicle of your life with *duty* rather than *gratitude*, you are heading for some kind of breakdown.

We know now that old paintings of the very first nativity are quite wrong. Mary and Joseph and the shepherds would have been there, but what you don't see is all their parents watching and filming it with cameras.

In Britain at Christmas many people still observe the tradition of going to see a performance with set responses and men dressed up as women …

Christmas today is as if someone's posted a private party on Facebook and now everyone's arrived and is smashing the place up.

Xmas

A gift is like a potted plant – it's pretty much up to me whether I feed, prune and harvest it. Or just let it die.

Repentance

Sometimes I feel that my conscience is like a basket of white socks that has been through the washing machine of repentance so many times that now everything's a bit grey.

Battle

In the spiritual battle of good versus evil how many good things would have to happen to you, to bribe you not to fight?

In the spiritual battle of good versus evil, how many bad things would have to happen to you, before you 'retire hurt'?

It's strange that we Christians can be so simplistic and prudish, because the book we bang on about is neither.

Perhaps try and see God's influence in the Bible, in the same way you would recognise a director's style when watching a season of their early films?

The Bible is like a little man with whom you wrestle regularly. He can be hard work, but often turns up to help you in a fight.

The Bible is hundreds of God's previous reactions to humanity. Absorb them enough and you'll begin to feel instinctively his reaction to you here and now.

What's rarely mentioned by either side in the women priests debate is that *it's not the most important thing.*

Commu

PLATITUDE EXCHANGE CENTRE

WHAT I THINK I'M SUPPOSED TO SAY

WHAT I THINK I'M SUPPOSED TO SAY IN RETURN

Ineffective preaching points to the colour and number of the door. Effective preaching unlocks it.

One of the most inspiring worship leaders there's ever been: David Attenborough.

Some Christians are against the culture of celebrity. Except when a celebrity becomes a Christian, of course. Then they want them to speak at all their meetings.

Opposition

If God is with you then the devil has the same power over you as a ghost train does. There'll be lots of bangs and crashes, none of which can touch you.

Christians often worry about the tiniest effect for bad of the occult on a person's life. But surely far more frightening is someone who has spent a lot of time in church, with no apparent effect for good.

The Devil can be a bit like someone called Ian. When people talk about him you think you know who they mean, but in reality they might be talking about someone else who they call Ian.

The Devil is in control of chaos. Or is he?

The Ten Commandments are not so much the safety instructions before take-off, but more like the scientific conditions required for flight itself.

(And if you keep breaking those rules you will begin to lose height and eventually crash down to earth.)

Dying

When we finally understand that God is paying the bill in this restaurant, some of us may wish we'd been a lot more audacious with what we asked for in the first place.

For Christians, life will be a lot like some of their meetings – much better when it's all over.

Heaven is the successful conclusion of a life trying to find God.

Hell is the successful conclusion of a life trying to avoid God.

Perhaps what happens after death is like being a footballer who either gets the nod to play in the first team … or is asked to leave the club.

Dying without faith will be like arriving for an exam you haven't revised for. Dying with faith will be like arriving for an exam, and finding out it's a prize-giving.

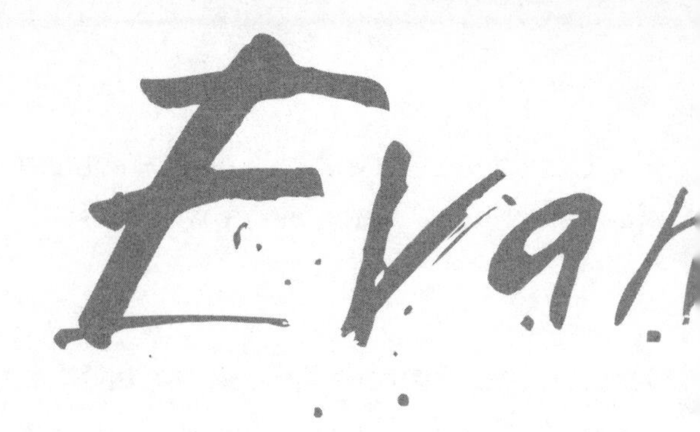

Sometimes I'm the type of Christian who mistakes exaggeration for evangelism. Oh yes, I forge links with neighbours, the local community, contacts all over the world … I forge all sorts of things.

It's easier to publicise a restaurant if you eat there regularly. And it's impossible to remain enthusiastic if you're just passing on other people's recommendations.

elism

'WE SHOULD ALWAYS BE RE-INVENTING CHRISTIANITY TO MAKE IT SIMPLER AND MORE RELEVANT _ WHICH IS WHY WE STARTED THE SEVEN NEW SPRINGS OF EPHESIANS 5 COMMUNITY WINESKIN PROJECT'

Forgiveness

People who forgive a big thing have usually forgiven many smaller things.

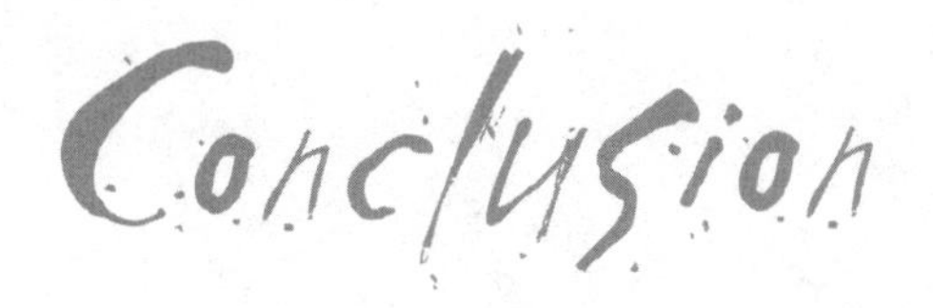

The DVD *The Universe* has a happy ending, but single frames won't make much sense. (You just get to play a pixel, btw.)

It's tempting to only start to pray to God when things take a big turn for the worse, but there may not even be time for introductions.

Best not point out the tiny scratch on my neighbour's car. Especially if it could have happened when mine was towed away, because it was abandoned long ago.

Hang On

Sometimes I stop and wonder if I'm making it all up, this climb up the mountain. But usually it just takes a quick look into the cold, unforgiving, hopeless abyss of the alternative to put me back on track.

Yes, and if I stay still long enough I can feel the peaceful power of it pushing me on up the path.

Christianity is not so much a religion, more the beginning of a realisation of how things really are.

This life only makes sense if it's 'Scene 1' of a much bigger production. (Maybe even only the audition.)

Yes, the only reason God can have allowed all the bad stuff is because the end result is worth it.

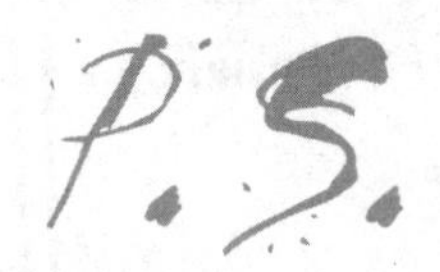

The whole truth is such a big lasagne, we can only really digest it in tiny mouthfuls of multi-layered allegory.

It's not just that God sees the 'big picture'. It's that the 'big picture' is on a wall, and that wall is in a room, in a house, on a street ... Yeah, it's all a lot bigger than anyone can ever think or imagine.